中国科幻小说精选 · 中英对照

温柔之乡的梦

DEAR DELUSION

魏雅华　著
温绍贤　译
［英］蒂娜·巴莱　审校

科学普及出版社
·北京·

图书在版编目（CIP）数据

温柔之乡的梦：中英对照/魏雅华著；温绍贤译．—北京：科学普及出版社，2014.6
（中国科幻小说精选）
ISBN 978-7-110-08626-1

Ⅰ．①温… Ⅱ．①魏… ②温… Ⅲ．①英语—汉语—对照读物 ②儿童文学—科学幻想小说—作品集—中国—当代 Ⅳ．①H319.4：I

中国版本图书馆CIP数据核字(2014)第096617号

出 版 人　苏　青
责任编辑　单　亭　张　莉
封面设计　银搏时代
责任校对　王勤杰
责任印制　张建农

出　　版　科学普及出版社
发　　行　科学普及出版社发行部
地　　址　北京市海淀区中关村南大街16号
邮　　编　100081
发行电话　010-62173865
传　　真　010-62179148
网　　址　http://www.cspbooks.com.cn

开　　本　880mm×1230mm　1/32
字　　数　41千字
印　　张　3.25
印　　数　1—5000册
版　　次　2014年8月第1版
印　　次　2014年8月第1次印刷
印　　刷　北京盛通印刷股份有限公司
书　　号　ISBN 978-7-110-08626-1 / H·211
定　　价　16.00元

CONTENTS

目录

结　局

我决定和我的机器人妻子离婚！

不管她怎样地用那泪水晶莹的、令人怜爱的眼睛恳求我的宽恕，不管她怎样用妻子的温柔和夫妻间特殊的词语来平息我的怒火，全是徒劳的。

曾几何时，我还认为我的婚姻是人世间最美满、最幸福的婚姻，可是……

我认定了，离婚！

事情是怎么发生的呢？

THE END

I have decided to divorce my robot wife.

She pleads for forgiveness, her pitiable and lovely eyes brimming with sparkling tears, and she tries to coax me out of my anger with her wifely tenderness and the special language used between husband and wife. But it's useless.

Before long, I had thought our marriage was the happiest on earth, but...

I maintain that I must divorce her.

What went wrong?

开　头

一年前，在我22岁生日的那天，我收到一张粉红色的、散发着麝兰香味的卡片。卡片是由婚姻管理中心寄来的。我可以凭这张卡片去我所愿意去的任何一家机器人公司，领取一位机器人姑娘作我的妻子。

我的家里有兄弟姊妹三人，我是最小的一个。由于我不是独生子女，按照人口法，我、哥哥、姐姐，三个人当中只有一个人可以与天然人结婚。根据优生学理论，为了避免人种退化，妇女享有特权，所以这个权利被我的姐姐获得了。我和哥哥法定应娶机器人妻子。

THE BEGINNING

A year ago, on my twenty-second birthday, I received an orchid-scented pink card from the Marriage Management Centre authorizing me to choose a robot wife. I could go to whichever of the robot companies I liked.

My parents have three children, two boys and a girl. I am the youngest. According to the Population Law only one of us has the right to marry a natural human being. In order to avoid degeneration of the race in the light of the theory of eugenics, females enjoy priority, so my sister is the one. My elder brother and I have to marry robot girls.

择 偶

我来到环球机器人公司。

总经理陪我进入机器人公司超级市场。看来这位总经理经营相当有方，他不是让这些机器人模特儿仅仅是站在那里供人们观赏挑选，而是让她们充当这里的售货员和服务员，供来客鉴赏。这个市场拥有1万名待嫁的机器人姑娘，姑娘同商品一起出售，不过姑娘要凭专用卡片。

直叫人目不暇接、眼花缭乱！

她们一个比一个美丽，你就像是进了百花争艳的花园。

这家公司是一流的，首先是因为这家公司拥有一批世界一流的、当代最杰出的美术家，拥有一支阵容强大、实力雄厚的，由画家、雕塑家、工艺美术家组成的美学家队伍；其次是由于他们拥有最完备的美学档案数据。他们拥有古代的和现代的、东方的和西方的、各种人种中最美丽的妇女造型的美学数据。

自从有史以来的四千年间，人类用恋爱这种手段来进

CHOOSING A WIFE

I went to Universal Robots Company.

The general manager took me to the company supermarket. He was evidently an experienced salesman for he did not just put the beautiful robot models on display for people to enjoy and to choose; he had them working in the supermarket as shop assistants and other staff attending to the customers who came to appreciate them. This supermarket has ten thousand robot girls in stock waiting for the right persons to choose them as wives, and they were sold together with other goods, but only for people holding the special cards.

There were too many of them for the eye to take in and I was simply dazzled by them.

Each one seemed more beautiful than the one before: it was like being in a park where the flowerbeds merge into an undifferentiated riot of colour.

It is a top-grade company. For one thing it employs the most prominent artistic designers of our time; they were all world-famous. Secondly, it has a strong lineup of talented aesthetic staff of painters, sculptors and industrial artists. It possesses the most perfect aesthetic modeling data on the most beautiful women of various races, ancient and modern, oriental and western.

During the four thousand years since the beginning of history, human beings have employed the method of love between

行一种美学法则的自然淘汰，但是进程相当缓慢，而且还常常受到权力与财产、政治与经济、傲慢与偏见等等各种因素的破坏和干扰。而现在，由于机器人的生产，这种进程可以用人的意志加以控制，在几个星期或几个月间的进步可能会超过几个世纪。

在环球机器人公司的档案里储存有西施、王昭君、杨玉环、赵飞燕、绿珠、莺莺、卓文君……这些东方古典型妇女造型的全部美学数据。

还有西方型的：如巴黎姑娘，也有吉卜赛女郎，有罗马型的，也有君士坦丁堡型的，有海仑娜那种仙女型的，也有莎士比亚笔下的苔丝特梦娜，或者普希金笔下的阿古丽娜那种传奇型的。

如果成型产品（她们各有千秋，独领风骚而绝不重复）还不能使您满意，那么别忙，可以定制。

您可以提出要求，这里具有所有最美丽的电影明星的美学档案，管理员可以为您提供索引。如果您在现实生活中（甚至您在街头、海滨、公园邂逅的）发现令您倾心喜

man and woman to conduct natural selection based on aesthetic law, but it has been a very slow process. Besides, it has always been damaged and interfered with by various factors such as power and property, politics and economics, pride and prejudice and so on. Now, since the appearance of robots, this process can be controlled by man's will, and the achievements in a few weeks or a few months can surpass those made in several centuries.

Stored in the archives of Universal Robots are all the vital statistics and specifications of oriental beauties of the past such as Xi Shi, Wang Zhaojun, Yang Yuhuan, Zhao Feiyan, Luzhu, Yingying, Zhuo Wenjun and so on.

There are also data of Western types: Parisiennes, gypsies, classical Roman women, Mediterranean charmers, other worldly types like Helena and romantics like Shakespeare's Desdemona and Pushkin's Akulena.

If none of these ready-made models (each has her strong points and her own lofty elegance having nothing in common with each other) appeals to you, you can have one made to order.

You can be quite specific. Aesthetic files are available – all indexed in great detail of the most beautiful actresses. Or you may have met a girl whose appearance inspired you in real life — in the street, on the seashore or in the park even. If

爱的少女容貌，只要您向这家公司提供线索，他们立刻会用极其巧妙的全息摄影取得所需要的全部美学数据，并且按照美学法则中的黄金分割比例加以鉴定、取舍，生产出您只有在梦中才能见到的、九天之上才有的、艳绝人寰的花容月貌，保证叫您爱不自禁，喜出望外！

总经理带着我从每一个柜台前慢慢地走过，让我充分地欣赏这些姑娘们的仙姿。

有一位艺术家说过：在一切自然形态中，最完美的是人。人是大自然的一件杰作。中国古人说，人是天地之灵秀，盖世之精华。看来这真是至理名言。

在宇宙间一切美的形态中、美的表现形式中，恐怕没有比人更美的了。

这些机器人姑娘像是蓓蕾初放的花朵，一朵比一朵娇美。总经理带着骄傲的口吻说："没有一个人不惊叹这些姑娘的美丽，因为她们是从世界上古今中外最美丽的人中'挑选'出来的佼佼者，群芳之冠。她们不仅令您悦目，而且还使您赏心。您的眼睛所能看到的还只是她们美的

you can provide enough information the company can immediately gather all the aesthetic specifications needed by means of a hologram very skillfully. The data will be analyzed and then it is decided which to use in accordance with the established principles of proportion and aesthetic law. The result will be a perfection you thought existed only in dreams or in the highest of heavens. You would of course fall instantly and passionately in love with her.

The general manager steered me from one counter to another, giving me enough time to appreciate the beauty of these girls in detail.

A certain artist once said that man is nature's sublime achievement: of all natural forms, man is the most perfect of all. There's a time-honoured Chinese adage about man being the intellect and cream of the universe.

Of all beauty forms and beauty shapes in the universe, no form or shape is more beautiful than that of man.

These robot girls are like fresh flower buds just breaking into bloom, with one more delicate and charming than the other. The general manager was saying proudly, "These girls with their charm and beauty are destined to win everybody's admiration; they are rare specimens, recreations of the most beautiful women the world has ever known—peerless champions. They are pleasing to both the eye and the mind. And you know it's not only what you can see: there's more to it

一部分——外在美，而她们还有更美的，可以使您受用终生、成为爱情之水永不枯竭的源头的内在美——性格的美。这些是您的眼睛所看不见的。中国古人把爱情比作一只玉环，玉者，取其洁白无瑕；环者，取其始终不断。而这恰恰可以用来形容机器人姑娘那天赋的对待爱情的忠贞性格。由于机器人姑娘的思维过程具有数学公式或几何定理那样简洁、明确、严格、单一的特性，所以她们毕生只爱一个人，谁的名字填写在她们的发货单据上，她的心里便永远只有这一个人，坚贞不二，生死不渝。”

我笑着问总经理：“如果我死了呢？”

总经理拍拍我的肩膀，“她是按照宇宙中的对称法则设计的，她的寿命与您的寿命是对称的。她的存在与您的存在是对称的，而您的死亡和她的死亡也是对称的。如同作用力与反作用力、向心力和离心力那样对称。您明白吗？”

我们慢慢地走着，观赏着这些奇妙的科学之花。

总经理微笑着向我介绍：“这还只是一个方面，还有另一个方面，这些姑娘不仅比鲜花还要美丽，而且比鲜

than that. What you can't see is their internal beauty — the perfect disposition which will inspire your love and keep you happy all your life. In ancient China people used to say love between a man and a woman was like a jade ring — jade for purity, the ring for eternity. This exactly describes our robot girls' attitude towards love. They are programmed with thought-processes as clear and direct and unalterable as a geometric theorem. They can only love one man. Once the purchaser's name is written on a robot girl's dispatch list, she will remain faithful to him till the day of her death."

"What if I die?" I asked with a smile.

The general manager patted me on the shoulder, "She is designed according to the universal law of symmetry, her life-span and existence corresponding to yours. While you live, she will live; when you die, she dies. The symmetry is like the compensating balance of applied force and reacting force, centripetal force and centrifugal force. Do you understand?"

We walked on slowly among the flower beds appreciating these wonderful scientific flowers.

The general manager went on smilingly, "This is only one side of the matter. On the other hand these girls are not only more beautiful but also more tender than fresh flowers. Your

花还要温柔，您未来的妻子不仅毕生不会和您打一次架，甚至连吵一次嘴都不会。”

“是吗？”我惊奇地问。因为据我所知，世界上几乎没有一对夫妻，哪怕是最和睦的夫妻，能够毕生不吵嘴的。而且据相关国际组织调查资料，在天然人的夫妻中离婚案件近年有增加的趋势。

“难道您不知道那个著名的机器人三定律吗？”总经理惊奇地瞅着我，仿佛我不知道地球是围绕太阳转的一样。于是，他向我指了指那矗立在整个超级市场中心的一座汉白玉雕砌玉碑，那块玉碑上雕着闪闪发光的美国人阿西莫夫的机器人三定律：

第一定律：机器人不得伤害人，也不得听任人受到伤害而无所作为。

第二定律：机器人应当服从人的一切命令，但不得违反第一定律。

第三定律：机器人应当保护自身安全，但不得违反第一、第二定律。

future wife won't even quarrel with you, let alone fight with you—not ever."

"Is that so?" I asked in amazement. As far as I knew no single couple had gone through life without a quarrel; even the most affectionate couples on earth quarreled sometimes. And according to a survey by the United Nations, divorce cases among human couples had increased in recent years.

"Don't you know the famous three laws of the robot?" The general manager stared at me in surprise, apparently wondering how I could be so ignorant. Then he pointed at a panel of white marble at the centre of the supermarket on which the three laws of the robot by Asimov were inscribed, glistening in the lights:

> **First law: A robot may not injure a human being or, through inaction, allow a human being to come to harm.**
>
> **Second law: A robot must obey the orders given it by human beings except where such orders could conflict with the First Law.**
>
> **Third law: A robot must protect its own existence as long as such protection does not conflict with the First and Second Laws.**

总经理说："这是我们机器人生产厂家的金科玉律。每一个机器人出厂都要经过这道极为严格的检验，如果哪家公司生产或漏检了违背这三个定律的产品，立刻就会被罚款、被关闭甚至受到法律制裁。"总经理指着第二定律的那一段"机器人应当服从人的一切命令"，对我说："您将成为她的君主，她将永远对您顺从，无限忠诚、无限信仰。她将会像您的手脚一样地听您使唤。她不是一个独立的人，她简直就是您身体的延续，无条件地服从您的一切命令。她是您的乐队，永远追随您的旋律，是您最优美的和声。她就像一只与您同频率的音叉，永远静听您的召唤，并且用完全相同的频率与您产生共鸣，单就这一点说，她有多么可爱！"

我走着、听着，听着、走着，像是在梦中，又像是在天上。总经理在我的耳边继续娓娓细说、侃侃而谈："天然人对您的指令有这样一组逻辑程序：指令信息—鉴别—决策（抗拒或执行）—行动，而机器人的逻辑程序却简单得多：

"We accept these laws as mandatory in manufacturing robots," the general manager told me. "Every robot has to undergo rigorous inspection in this respect when leaving the factory. Any company producing robots which infringes these laws or fails to conduct proper inspections in accordance with these laws will be fined or closed down or even punished by law." Pointing to the second law—A robot must obey the orders given it by human beings—he assured me, "You will become her master—you might even say her ruler—and she will be obedient to you, be loyal and faithful to you forever. She will serve you like your own hands and feet. She won't seem like an independent person but simply an extension of your own body and obey all your orders unconditionally. She is your band, and she will ever provide perfect harmony to your melody. Like a tuning fork she will vibrate to your frequency. She will forever listen attentively to your call and resonate with you with the frequency completely identical to yours. You see what a paragon you will have!"

I was in a daze, yet listening to the general manager's voice rattling on in my ear, " The natural person reacts to an instruction by the following logical programme: instructive information—appraisal—decision (to implement it or not) —action. But the robot's logical programme is much simpler and more concise:

“指令—执行。

“因为她的软件就是这样设计的，所以她永远不会对您变心，你们虽然是两个人，却只有一个脑袋，这不正符合那奇妙的爱情公式：

“1 + 1 = 1！

了吗……

“小伙子，这样的妻子，难道不正是理想的化身？”

“可她不会生育！”我嘟囔了一句。

“您哪！”总经理冲着我嘲笑地点了点头：“这难道是她的短处吗？这恰恰是她的长处！您不要忘记：她不会衰老！她永远是妙龄女郎，永远青春长驻。要孩子干什么呢？养儿防老吗？您别忘记，女儿要嫁走，她心里常常只装着她的丈夫；儿子也常常会娶了媳妇忘了娘。可妻子却大不相同，只有她是最忠诚的。她会忠心耿耿地侍奉您，直到您寿终正寝的那天。她既具有您妻子的身份，又兼备您的儿女的功能，天底下哪有这样尽善尽美的妻子？说到儿女，生儿育女又是多么辛苦的一件事！虽然孩子能给家

"instruction — implementation.

"Robot software is designed like that. Therefore your robot wife will never cease to be faithful to you. You are two persons but you'll have only one mind. You will be in perfect conformity with the wonderful love formula:

"1 + 1 = 1!

"My lad, don't you think a wife like her is just the ideal incarnate?"

"But she is unable to bear children," I muttered.

"Now really...!" He looked reprovingly at me. "Is that a defect? Of course not; it's one of her good points. Remember, she will never get old and feeble! She will stay young, always in the bloom of youth. What do you want children for anyway? To look after you when you are old? Don't forget that when your daughter marries she will always think first of her husband. As for sons — sons often forget their parents when they marry. But with a wife it's quite different, she will be faithful to you and look after you devotedly until you die in bed of old age. She will be both a wife and a daughter to you. Could you find a more perfect wife on earth? As to this matter of child bearing, it's a laborious business! I don't deny that children can bring joy to a family, but they bring a lot of hard work and poverty and endless worries. They would take up all

庭带来乐趣，可更多的是操劳、贫穷和苦累，他将会耗费您多少宝贵的精力！再说，如果您在晚年，在精神上确实需要这么一个小把戏——儿子或女儿——他们对您就像一个活的玩具。到那时候您来，我们会给您提供一个机器人的孩子，儿子还是女儿由您选择，他（她）既具有您的遗传因子，又具有您妻子的遗传因子，而且是取两者之优。您只要一见到这个小家伙，就绝不会相信他（她）是一个小机器人，您一定会认为这是您寄放在托儿所的孩子，或者是您失散了的骨肉……说到机器人不会生育，但她却有她伟大的历史功勋。正是由于机器人不会生育，才解决了从20世纪60年代开始的世界性的人口危机，使这几十年来世界人口始终维持在40亿左右，避免了由于人口过剩而导致的通货膨胀、经济危机、饥饿、动乱、战争……以及由于人口危机而导致的世界灾难性的总崩溃，从这一点来说，简直是机器人拯救了人类。难道，您能说，这是她的短处吗？”

我哑口无言。

岂止是哑口无言，而且是几乎不会说话了！

your energy. And—by the way—if you really want to have such a plaything morally in your old age—a son or a daughter—(he or she is just like a toy having life to you by then) then come back to me and we will contrive a robot child for you, son or daughter, whichever you like. He or she would have both your and your wife's genetic factors based on optimization. I can tell you—when you see such a little child you wouldn't believe it was a little robot. You'd really think it was your own child brought up in the nursery or your own flesh and blood restored to you after years of separation... You said just now that the robot girl was unable to bear children. True, but that has not prevented her from performing a considerable historical service for mankind. It's precisely because the robots are unable to have children that the problem of world population crisis, which began in the 1960's of the twentieth century, has been solved. For some decades now the population of the world has remained stable at around four billion. As a result the problems of inflation, economic crisis, starvation, turmoil and war have ceased to plague us. We are no longer haunted by the fear of a worldwide catastrophic collapse of civilization as a result of over-population. In this sense we may say the robot has saved mankind. Can you really say it's a defect?"

I was rendered speechless.

I was not only speechless but I almost couldn't speak.

因为我发现了她——丽丽！

这是我无法解释的，我也不明白我为什么，又怎么会在这万花丛中一下就认定了她！

可是那位总经理还在滔滔不绝地讲呢："也正是由于机器人不会生育，所以我们的公司才能存在。不然，天然人姑娘早把我们公司捣成一座废墟了。她们嫉妒机器人姑娘，因为比她们更漂亮，天然人望尘莫及。如果机器人姑娘再会生育，那么天然人姑娘就会无地自容，就会有被淘汰的危险。正因为她们不会生育，天然人姑娘才会有资格翘着鼻子嗤笑她们：'瞧那些不会下蛋的母鸡！'正是由于她们不会生育，天然人姑娘才会具有申请配给的特权。不过天然人姑娘也能和机器人姑娘和睦相处，甚至亲如姐妹。因为机器人姑娘特别本份，绝对不会去勾引她们的丈夫。机器人姑娘对自己的丈夫是一团火，而对别的男人是一块冰，她们会勇敢地保卫自己的贞操不受侵犯，因为在机器人三定律中有进行自卫的条款……走呀，小伙子。"这时他才发现我远远地落在他后面了。

Because I had discovered her—Lily.

I was unable to give an explanation. I don't know why I chose her from among the ten thousand flowers at a glance!

The general manager's tide of eloquence flowed on, "It's precisely because the robot girls are unable to bear children that our company can exist. Otherwise human girls would have wrecked it long ago. They are jealous of the robot girls for they are far more beautiful than they. If the robot girls could bear children, the human girls would feel themselves inferior and also feel their very existence was threatened, but now that they can't bear children, the human girls are in a position to be swollen with arrogance and sneer at the robots as 'hens that can't lay eggs'. This is why the human girls find themselves in the privileged position of being rationed in response to applications. Another thing—human girls can get on well with robot girls like sisters because the robot girls particularly behave well and would never try to seduce their husbands. Robot girls are warm and loving to their own husbands but like ice to other men. Of course, they will defend their chastity; you remember the self defence clause in the Third Law...Hullo, what's happened to you?" He suddenly noticed I had lagged behind.

择偶

在出售名酒的柜台后面伫立着一位天仙。现在她正出神地望着对面柜台旁边那一个一个的大鱼缸，那些美丽的金鱼和光彩夺目的燕鱼正在争夺鱼食。

我真无法形容她的美丽，最华美的词藻在她的面前都显得很徒劳！我只感到，当我第一眼看到她的时候，我的全身、我的血液，就像一团饱和的酒精蒸气，碰到了跳跃着、燃烧着的火苗，“砰！”的一声，烧起来了！我的全身、我的血液、我的每一根毛发都在燃烧！都在燃烧中颤栗！

莫非，这就是爱情的滋味？……看一眼就会着火，看一眼就会醉倒？！

她却完全没有看见我，她正在凝视着那些金鱼，长长的睫毛下“星星”正在闪耀，皓月般的脸蛋儿上一双笑窝儿若隐若现。那神态，是喜悦？是娇媚？是向往？是猜度？……她就像伫立在喷水池中美玉雕琢成的塑像，全身都挂着露珠儿在闪光。

她是姑娘里的太阳，她是太阳里的姑娘！

Behind the wine counter stood this goddess. She was gazing at a large fish tank near the counter, lost in thought. The golden carp and other bright platax teira jostled each other for the food.

Her beauty was beyond description—no words could do justice to her. At first sight of her I seemed to catch fire — my blood, my whole body were alight with fire. It was a feeling that made me quiver with intense excitement, which could only be sensed, but could not be explained by words.

Was it love? I was intoxicated from the first glance at her.

She didn't notice me in the least. She was watching the fish. Her eyes shone like diamonds under her long lashes, and she had enchanting little dimples on her face which was like a shining moon... What does this look mean? Is it joy? Coquettishness? Yearning for something? Or conjecture? ... I saw her as a jade statue standing at the centre of the fountain in the shimmering radiance of spray.

She was the sun of the girls; she was the girl in the sun.

……

总经理一眼就明白了是怎么回事，他走到我身边亲热地拍了拍我的肩膀，笑着说：“好，有眼力，小伙子！她是我们本年度获得金质奖的最佳作品，归你了！”

他立刻拿出笔来，在那张卡片上签上了丽丽的名字。然后，叫了一声：“丽丽！”我想阻止都没来得及。

丽丽吃了一惊，她抬起头来，那双动人的眼睛闪动着惊诧的光彩，她看到总经理带着一位容光焕发的小伙子向她走来，她立刻羞得满脸通红，埋下头去，再也不敢抬起，旁边的一些姑娘都窃窃地笑出声来。

总经理走到她面前，把那张浅红色的卡片交给她，然后对她说：“把手伸出来！”

我看见她的头一直低垂到胸前，垂着那长长的睫毛，看也不敢看我一眼，像是羞得无地自容，乖乖地伸出了那纤巧细柔的小手。

总经理从口袋里掏出一只首饰盒子，取出一对订婚戒

...

The general manager immediately grasped what had happened. He came over to me and patted my shoulder warmly, saying genially, “Well, you’ve got very good judgment, my lad! She is our company’s gold-medalist this year. Now she’s yours!”

He promptly took out his pen and wrote Lily’s name on my card. Then he called, “Lily!” It was too late for me to stop him.

She raised her head, startled, her charming eyes wide with surprise. On seeing that the general manager was bringing a smart young man to her she immediately blushed and hung her head. The girls around her giggled.

The general manager went to her and handed her the pink card. Then he said, “Stretch out your hand, please!”

She kept her head bent and her eyes with long lashes cast down, not daring to look at me and she was so shy that she looked as if she wished she could disappear from view. Obediently she stretched out her delicate little hand.

The general manager pulled a jewel case from his pocket,

指，庄重地把镶有红宝石的一枚戴在我的手上，把镶有绿猫眼的一枚戴在她的手上。

姑娘们都围了过来，笑着，叫着，推搡着。戒指刚刚戴好，欢呼声、音乐声立刻四起，花雨像瀑布一样倾泻下来，玫瑰、茉莉、丁香、红梅、蔷薇……红的、黄的、紫的、白的……各种各样的花瓣洒落了一身一地，男女傧相拥向我和丽丽，我们被分别送去更衣沐浴换装。

不一会儿，当我再看到丽丽的时候，她已经剪掉了那标志姑娘身份的长辫，披着美丽的卷发，穿着结婚的纱裙，亭亭玉立地站在我的面前。

环球机器人公司立刻播发了我们结婚的电视新闻。

我们在喜庆的音乐声中被簇拥着送出大门，我的汽车早已被披红戴绿地打扮过了。

总经理在我的前额和她的前额上都轻轻地吻了一下，他喜欢这古老的礼节，然后祝福我们："祝你们相亲相爱，白头偕老！"

opened it and took out two betrothal rings. He solemnly put the ruby one on my finger and the cat's eye one on hers.

The girls crowded round us, laughing and pushing.

No sooner had the rings been put on our fingers than cheers and music arose all round us. Flowers rained down on us—roses, jasmine, lilac, plum blossom...red, yellow, violet, white...cascaded from our hair and shoulders till we stood in a fragrant, multi-coloured sea of petals. The best man and the bridesmaid came to embrace us and then lead us away to take a bath and be decked up in wedding finery.

Later, when Lily and I met again, her long braid which signified her unmarried status had been cut off. She stood before me, slim and graceful, in her filmy wedding gown with her hair lying in soft curls on her shoulders.

Universal Robots immediately broadcast the news of our wedding over the TV networks.

We were escorted to the entrance to the sound of jubilant music. My car had already been decorated with red silk flowers and green leaves.

The general manager softly kissed us both on the forehead. It was easy to see that he enjoyed this traditional ceremony. Then he blessed us: "May you love each other dearly and remain a devoted couple to the end of your lives!"

坐在车上，我看了一眼丽丽，她正好也转过脸来偷偷地看我，她的目光正碰上我的目光，她羞得像被火烫了似地哆嗦了一下，赶快掉过头去。

我，已经醉了。

When we were in the car I looked at Lily and found she was just turning her head to steal a glance at me. Our eyes met and she was so shy that she trembled as if she had been burnt by fire. She quickly turned her head away.

I felt light-headed with happiness.

蜜　月

燕尔新婚、初结伉俪的幸福真是难以形容。

她的美丽使你只要看上一眼，就会掉进爱情的深渊。我常常工作到深夜，她总是与我守灯相伴，只要我抬起眼皮一看到丽丽，我的疲劳立刻就会烟消云散。这时我的心头就会浮起那一句优美的古老诗行：

“红袖添香夜读书。”

大概是因为我的眼里常常洋溢着那么多的爱恋，她的眼里才常常闪烁着幸福的羞怯。现在我才理解了总经理向我介绍的“鲜花般的美丽、鲜花般的温柔”话中深刻的内涵。丽丽的性格比她的外表还要美丽，她对我真是百依百顺，她的模样儿像天仙，她的性格像天使。

她是那样聪明，她那双美丽清澈、一池春水般的眼睛一眼就能看透我的心，我才刚刚想到的，她就已经为我做好了。我简直觉得我们之间那种浓郁的爱、那种馨芳的爱已经达到了饱和……

HONEYMOON

Our newly married life was a blissful beginning.

I had only to look at her to be transported into an ecstasy of love. I often worked far into the night and she would keep me company sitting by me in the circle of light. Whenever I raised my head and saw Lily, my fatigue would completely vanish. I was reminded of an elegant line from an ancient Chinese poem:

"The night-reading scholar, with a red-robed girl adding in more sandalwood to the incense burner. "

Probably owing to my eyes always filled with so much love and devotion, her eyes often glistened with happiness and bashfulness. Now I understood the general manager's profound intension when he said that she was "more beautiful and more tender than fresh flowers. " Lily's disposition was indeed even more beautiful than her appearance. She was gentle and compliant; her appearance was like that of a goddess and her disposition like that of an angel.

Her quick, receptive intelligence and her beautiful limpid eyes saw straight into my mind at a glance. I would think of something I wanted and she would do it before I had said a word. I simply felt that our deep and fragrant love had reached the point of saturation...

我们之间，我象征着权威，她象征着服从。我现在才领会到总经理所说的“您就是她的君主”这句话那深刻的含义、那美妙的滋味。

我现在才认识到那个计算爱情的奇妙公式：

$$1+1=1$$

它是何等正确！

尤其是它对于我们夫妻比对于其他任何一对夫妻来说都更加深刻，更加富有哲理。因为我们两个人只有一个脑袋，那就是我的脑袋，我是歌唱家，她是我的乐队；我是电视台，她是电视机，而且只有一个频道，我播什么，她收什么。

我们之间在进行着一种奇妙的循环，这种循环可以用牛顿的万有引力定律来加以阐述。牛顿定律中说：“引力的大小与距离的平方成反比”。那么，也就是说，距离越小，引力越大，而引力越大，距离就越小。这样向心力在急剧地按平方关系递增，距离却在急剧地按平方关系递减。这就是我们之间爱情关系的数学公式。

I symbolized authority and she obedience. The general manager's remark about me becoming her master came back to me and I now knew what he meant. I revelled in the meaning.

I understood, too, the wonderful love formula:

$$1 + 1 = 1$$

What an accurate formula!

I felt that it was uniquely applicable to us and more philosophical to us — that more than any other couple in the whole world. We were truly of one heart and one mind—my heart and my mind. I was a singer while she was my band; I was a TV station with only one channel while she was a TV set, and she just listened to what I broadcast.

A wonderful attraction vibrated between us. This attraction could be expounded by Newton's law of universal gravitation which says that the force of gravitation "is inversely proportional to the square of distance". Indeed, the shorter the distance is, the greater the gravitation. The greater the gravitation is, the shorter the distance and the shorter the distance, the greater the gravitation, thus the centripetal force drastically increases by degrees according to square function and the distance drastically decreases by degrees in the same way. This was the mathematic formula of love between Lily and me.

蜜月

只有热恋中的情人，才能体会到牛顿定律的神威。牛顿在提出他这条不朽的公式的时候，大概没想到它也适用于计算爱情。

有人说结婚是爱情的终结，看来这话片面了。结婚是爱情的更高阶段。

在这一段时间里，我的工作也特别顺利，“POT”研究计划正在乘风破浪、势如破竹般地长驱直入，它就快要结出丰硕的果实了。在这个时候，我特别想念这项工作的奠基人——我的老师史纯教授，也想起了他临终时千叮万嘱的遗言——“一定要把109号元素找到！”

现在，全世界的重离子物理学界都在这条跑道上冲刺，只要我们再加把劲，就会捷足先登、胜券在握！

可是……唉！

Only people head over heels in love could realize the potent force of this law of Newton's. When he propounded it he probably never imagined it was also applicable to the calculation of love.

Some people hold that marriage is the end of love. That was a warped view. I firmly believed that marriage was the higher phase of love.

During this period my work was going particularly smoothly. The POT research programme was progressing so easily and successfully that a rich harvest would soon be reaped. At this time, I cherished more than ever the memory of the founder of the programme, my revered teacher Professor Shi Chun, and of his deathbed injunction: "Element 109 must be found!"

Now, in heavy ion research laboratories across the world, physicists were putting on a spurt towards the tape. If we had that vital bit of energy in reserve, we could win.

But...Alas!

温柔之乡

在这一段时间里，我的眼睛只能看到她的长处，她具有天然人姑娘的一切优点，她几乎摒弃了天然人姑娘的一切缺点，她在我的眼里简直就是个尽善尽美的、天仙般的、超理想化的妻子。

她对我的顺从已经到了无以复加的地步。在这一点上，她具有浓厚的东方妇女的特色。像是中国古代的妇女，或者日本、朝鲜的女性，她不仅无条件地接受我的一切指令，连我的恶作剧也逆来顺受。

我想要试验一下她的顺从究竟能达到怎样的地步，我想了一些小小的花样来对她进行测试。

例如：吃过饭，偏不让她洗碗碟。我笑着说："丽丽，舔净。"

她乖乖地拿过盘子，瞅着我，像是希望我改变指令，却装作没听清。

我偏不！

THE LAND OF HEART'S DESIRE

During that early period, what I came to know were her good points. She possessed all the virtues of human girls but none of their defects. To me, she was simply a perfect and super-ideal wife who was also as beautiful as a goddess.

She was obedient to me in the extreme. In this sense she was typical of oriental women—of Chinese women in ancient times, of Japanese and Korean women. She carried out all my instructions unconditionally and, what was more, she submitted meekly to my malicious provocation.

To test the degree of her submission I thought of some tricks.

For example, once, when we had finished our meal I stopped her washing the bowls and plates. Then I smiled and said, "Lily, lick them clean."

She obediently took a plate in her hand and looked enquiringly at me, in the hope that I would change my instruction. She pretended that she hadn't heard me clearly.

But I didn't relent.

我又说一遍，带着央求："丽丽，舔净。"

她只好拿起盘子，像只猫一样，伸出小舌头，带着响声，舔着盘子上的残屑。一双眼睛委屈地瞅着我。

我呢，还她一个笑——一个顽皮的、得意的、满足的笑。

她也乐了。

一会儿，我又变个花样。我说："丽丽，学猫叫。"

这回她不再为难了，只是埋怨地瞅我一眼，像是说："就你花样多！"然后，做个鬼脸，就"喵—，喵—"地叫起来，像是真的小猫儿一样。

可我对她的每一个服从都以更热烈的爱作为报答。于是，我们之间的这种权威与服从就越发牢固了。

我们经常在一起对弈，她的棋术相当高明，因为她读过好几本棋谱。可她从来不敢赢我，我要悔棋、赖子，她总是带着埋怨的微笑瞅着我，从来不敢顶嘴，而且总是一边下棋一边偷看我的脸色。一看我的脸色不对便赶紧设法故意走错棋、错步，好让我挽回败局，转败为胜，笑逐颜开。

开始，她的温柔宽厚很得我的欢心。但时间一长，我

I repeated steadily, "Lily, lick them clean, please. "

She had no choice but to put out her tongue like a cat and lick the messy plate, making lapping noises as she did so. She looked at me all the time, aggrieved.

I gave her a smile in return, a mean, triumphant, smug smile.

She seemed grateful even for that.

On another occasion I said to her, "Lily, please mew like a cat. "

She didn't hesitate this time. With a reproachful look which seemed to say, "What are you up to this time?" she made a wry face and uttered the sound "mew, mew", very cat-like.

I always rewarded her submission with fervent demonstrations of love. As a result, our relationship of authority and submission grew stronger all the time.

We often played Chinese chess. She had read a whole lot of manuals and was an expert player. But she never dared to beat me. If I retracted a false move in the game she would look at me with a reproachful smile but she never dared argue with me. Moreover, when we were playing, she would dart a quick glance at my face, and if she found me looking moody or bad-tempered, she would quickly and deliberately make a wrong move so that I could be saved from defeat and win the game which cheered me up at once.

All this was blissful... at first. However, as time went by I

就感到厌倦了。我这时才体会到似乎吵架也是一种乐趣。就像月亮要有阴晴圆缺，季节要有春夏秋冬一样。就像一个厌恶夏天太热、冬季太冷的人，好不容易才迁居到一个四季如春的地方，却又感到这个地方的季节未免过于单调，不如原来所住的地方那样四季分明，丰富多彩。

我想故意惹她生气，看她生不生气！

早上，我把脚一伸，她赶快给我穿上袜子、鞋子。穿好衣服后，她赶快给我洗脸，刮胡子。她正刮着我打了一个喷嚏，小刀把我的脸碰破了个口子。我气愤了，抬手就是一巴掌，她乖乖地站着挨打，打了这边脸蛋儿，又把那边脸蛋儿送过来。眼里噙着泪水，脸上还赔着笑。

瞧瞧，就这么乖！

我也真的很爱她。

我就不信她不生气，兔子急了还咬人呢！

我故意找茬儿，一转身把一只水晶杯子碰掉在地上，打碎了。我立刻大发脾气，骂她没长眼睛，放的不是地方，还专拣能刺激她的话骂，骂她臭机器人，骂她没爹没妈没

began to weary of it. It occurred to me that quarrelling, too, provides a certain pleasure. The full moon and the waning moon complement one another; so do the seasons. A man who tries to escape from the extremes of summer and winter into endless spring will eventually tire of its monotony and lack of variety and long for change.

I set about trying to make her angry.

It happened one morning. First I stuck my feet out at her to oblige her to put my socks and shoes on for me. After I had dressed she would wash my face and shave me. I sneezed and the razor made a small cut. I flew into a rage and slapped her face, but all she did was to stand there unprotestingly and even turn her other cheek to me to be slapped. Her eyes filled with tears but she summoned up a conciliatory smile.

What a doormat she was!

Of course, I really loved her dearly.

But I didn't believe she would ever get angry. Even a rabbit will bite in the end.

I made a point of placing obstacles in her way. I knocked a crystal glass on to the floor and broke it and then bawled at her and blamed her for putting it in the wrong place. I deliberately used provocative language to abuse her, saying she was a disgusting robot and had no parents to educate

教养……

她呢，眼泪一串一串地往下掉，嘴里一边认错，手里一边收拾。我心疼了，又赶快甜言蜜语地哄她，直到她笑出声儿来。

你有什么法儿呢？

她就是不生气！

我到现在才体会到阿西莫夫三定律的威力。

她从制造出来就没学会顶嘴、吵架。她就是顺从的化身。她是用顺从的水掺和着顺从的土合成的顺从的泥巴。她是用99个顺从加1个顺从做成的性格。

可是我却有了变化。

我的脾气越来越坏。而且由于我在家里是个专制的君王，我在外面就感到事事不顺心，看谁都不顺眼。在研究所、在实验室、在服务部，那些天然人使我越来越感到他们粗鲁、放肆、野蛮、傲慢、骄横、丑陋不堪。我越觉得丽丽可爱，就越觉得他们可恶，我离丽丽越近，离他们就越远。

her...

And she? With tears pouring down her face as she cleared up the broken glass, she admitted that it was all her fault. Then I was overcome with remorse and found myself coaxing and teasing her until finally I managed to make her laugh.

What to do next?

She wouldn't get angry.

At this point I grasped the full significance of Asimov's laws.

The ability to answer back and quarrel had not been built into her when she was manufactured. She was the embodiment of submission, made of submissive clay mixed with submissive water. Her disposition was composed of 99 molecules of submission plus one molecule of submission.

However, I had changed a lot.

I became more and more bad tempered. As I grew into my role of despot at home, I found the world outside less and less to my liking. Everyone seemed offensive. It was the same at the institute: in the lab., in the service section, the natural people I had known now appeared to me to be uncouth, arrogant, overbearing and ugly. Lily's loveliness made everyone else repulsive by contrast. The more I got close to Lily, the more I kept a distance with these people.

这样，我越来越喜欢待在家里，越来越感到办公室肮脏、杂乱、空气污浊。我在研究所里的时间越来越少了。

昨天上午，我开着汽车进入市区，进入商业区后，道路变得狭窄了。我直按喇叭，前面的那辆车就是不肯让路。我气愤了，加速超车，没想到碰了左面的一辆车，结果擦掉了我车上的一块漆皮。我停下车来，与那辆车上的人大吵了一通。警察反而罚了我的款。

我的上级找我谈话，对我进行了批评。指出我一年来变得懒、横、傲、燥、怪癖。并说，这是我结婚以后发生的变化。还向我严肃地指出，目前“POT”研究计划即将瓜熟蒂落，全所的研究人员都在日夜兼程、加倍努力，我作为项目的主要负责人，这种精神状态是不能允许的。

我一肚子的火：是他们嫉妒我妻子的美丽、贤惠？还是他们嫉妒我美满幸福的家庭？

丽丽有什么错呢？

可怜的丽丽！我逐渐地感觉到天然人和机器人之间的本质区别——他们的灵魂是大不相同的。

So I liked to stay at home more than ever, away from the squalor, confusion and dirty air of the office, and spent less and less time at the institute.

In one morning, I drove the car into town. The streets seemed narrower and I kept my thumb on the horn, but the car ahead of me wouldn't let me pass. I lost my temper and accelerated, determined to overtake him, but I misjudged it and shaved the other car on the left so that my car was scratched. I stopped and got out and had a terrific row with the other driver. But the police fined me.

My supervisor sent for me and criticized me. He said that in the past year I had become lazy, supercilious and unpredictable and that all this had happened since my marriage. He pointed out seriously that the POT research programme was in its final stages and as all the staff of the institute were working day and night to finish it, it was unacceptable for me, as the person in charge of the programme, to indulge in such eccentric behaviour.

I was exasperated. Were they jealous of me for having a beautiful and virtuous wife? Or were they jealous of me for having a happy family?

What had Lily done wrong?

Poor Lily! I gradually perceived the essential distinction between human beings and robots—their souls are immeasurably different.

现在，牛顿定律的另一半在我和他们之间也在起作用了：距离越远、引力越小；引力越小呢，距离越远。引力在按平方关系急剧衰减，距离在按平方关系急剧加大。

向心力在我与丽丽之间递增，离心力在我与研究所之间递增。一个恶性循环，一个良性循环，两个循环都在以平方关系的速度激化。速度越来越快，都在向着临界点发展。

对我的这次批评不但没有使我清醒，反而使我与同事们、与领导之间的关系更加疏远了，它甚至影响到了我的哲学思想，使我对天然人、对人类社会的前景产生了怀疑。使我变成了一个悲观论者和怀疑论者。

我甚至认为有一天，天然人将会被聪明而美丽的并且越来越先进的机器人所淘汰，要知道天然人的换代、进步，要比机器人的换代、进步慢得多。人类踏着缓慢而沉重的步子走了四千年，才有了今天的智力水平，而第一代计算机从问世到现在，全部历史才只有几十年，就已经赶上甚至超过了现代人的智力水平。且机器人的生育、死亡、

Now this alienation from my colleagues clearly illustrated another point in Newton's law: the longer the distance is, the smaller the gravitation; the smaller the gravitation, the longer the distance. Gravitation was decreasing drastically according to square function while distance was increasing drastically to the same extent.

Centripetal force between me and Lily and centrifugal force between me and the institute were increasing proportionately to one another. One was a vicious circle and the other a benign circle, both intensifying at the speed of square function. As the speed increased, disaster became inevitable.

The criticism had not sobered me up. On the contrary, it made me worse: I became further estranged from my colleagues and from the leadership. Even my philosophic thinking was affected and I began to have doubts about the future of human beings and human society. I became a pessimist and a sceptic.

I even inclined to the belief that human beings would in the end be replaced by the intelligent and beautiful robots which were becoming ever more and more advanced. The evolutionary progress of human beings is far slower than the technological development of the robots. Mankind has attained today's intellectual level by shuffling painfully forwards for thousands of years, but in the few decades since the first primitive electronic computer came into being it has caught up with and surpassed the intellectual performance of modern man. Moreover, the production, death, planning, management, quantity and quality and design can all be controlled

规划、管理，数量和质量的控制、设计，要比天然人容易得多。机器人是那样聪明、善良、驯服，又那样容易进行统治，永远不会爆发战争和骚乱，不会有阴谋、颠覆和政变，不需要军队和暴力，可以节省天文数字般庞大的军费开支……

我的结论是：迟早有一天，天然人将会被机器人所淘汰，人类社会将会发生本质的变化，在这场生存竞争中，人类将彻底失败。

我在温柔之乡中沉沦。

much easier for robots than for human beings. The robots are so clever, good-natured, even-tempered and so biddable that there would never be wars, disturbances, conspiracies, subversions, or coup d'états. No armies or violence would be needed, so the enormous figures of military expenditure could therefore be saved...

Yes, I finally came to the conclusion that the robots would ultimately take over and fundamental changes would take place in human society. Mankind would be overwhelmed in the struggle for survival and human society would be phased out.

I sank into degradation in the land of heart's desire.

沉　沦

事情不断地在发展变化。现在，我得回顾一下最近发生的一系列事情。

我本来是烟瘾很大的，后来，我发现吸烟严重损害我的健康，特别是引起我的支气管炎，于是我开始控制吸烟量。我买了一个特制的烟盒，这个烟盒有计时装置，每两小时才能吐出一支烟。这样，我就可以把我的吸烟量压缩到每天四到五支。

采取了这个措施之后，我的健康状况确有好转。但是，我也得承认，这个办法也常常憋得我难受。有时我也常常对着这个吝啬的烟盒叹气。

细心的丽丽发现了我的这个秘密。

于是她悄悄地找到烟盒的钥匙，悄悄地把钥匙带在身边，看到我对着烟盒发愁的时候，就悄悄地把钥匙放在我的面前，用那双钻石般的黑眼睛悄悄地在一旁观察我的脸色。

瞧瞧！这么好的媳妇，这么讨人疼爱的媳妇，还有什

DEGRADATION

To show how the situation was beginning to develop, I would like now to relate some events which took place recently.

I had been a heavy smoker. Lately, when I realized that smoking was injuring my health and giving me bronchitis, I began to cut down. I bought a special cigarette box with a timing device which let out one cigarette every two hours. In this way I could limit my smoking to five cigarettes a day.

This certainly did my health good but I must admit that I found it pretty trying. Sometimes I would sigh as I looked longingly at this stingy cigarette box.

My ever-thoughtful Lily discovered my secret.

Consequently, she hunted for the key and found it and kept it with her. When she saw that I was craving for a cigarette she silently laid the key in front of me and stood watching me with those diamond-like dark, intense eyes.

You see what a dear, good wife she was! But I really shouldn't

么可挑剔的呢?

还有呢!

酒是我心爱的饮料，离了它我就活不成。但如同吸烟一样，我喝得很有节制、很谨慎，只在每天中午喝两小杯淡淡的葡萄酒。

我深知生命现象无一不是电的运动形式，人体的超微弱发光、生物电、生物磁场、人体的特异功能，都是生物电的表现形式。我之所以对酒有特别的感情，正是基于上述理论。饮酒对我，就像是电池的充电。我也明白，电流太大会危及线圈，造成大脑节律放电并危及心脏。所以，我也严格控制酒量。

可是……要知道，美酒有多么诱人！那醇香、那甘美、那刺激、那兴奋……反正，爱酒的人谁都知道，那诱惑力实在难以抵御！

我的这点嗜好当然也逃不过她那充满着爱的眼睛。

晚饭的时候，我看到她亲手烹调的精美菜肴，不由得一双眼睛就转向那食品橱里的酒瓶，心里想，要是能再喝

nitpick.

That wasn't the only thing.

Wine is my favourite drink and I simply couldn't live without it. As with smoking, I was moderate and cautious in drinking, having only two small glasses of light grape wine at lunch every day.

I knew very well that all biological phenomena were manifestations of electricity and that ultra-faint luminescence, bioelectricity, biomagnetic field and the unusual functions of the human body were evidence of bioelectricity. That I had a special affection for wine was based on just the above theory—wine to me was as current charge to a battery. Of course I knew too strong an electric current would damage the coil which would cause a discharge in the rhythm of the cerebrum. That meant getting drunk and posing a threat to the heart. For this reason I strictly limited my intake of liquor.

But...we all know what a temptation good wine is! Its mellowness, its sweetness, its stimulus, its excitability... Those who are fond of wine know how irresistible it can be.

Naturally my addiction to wine hadn't escaped Lily's loving eyes.

In the evenings, when I saw the delicious dishes she had cooked for dinner, my eyes would turn unvoluntarily to the cupboard where the bottle of wine lived and I would think if only

上两杯，该多好啊！

又被她猜中了。她伸手拿过酒瓶，于是……我每餐都离不开她了。笑声在餐桌边多了，丽丽的眼泪也常常伴随着笑声洒落。

丽丽发现我的笑的频度是与食品橱内库存的酒量成反比的，她为这个发现十分得意。

可她和我都没有注意到那潜伏着的危机，这个危机正在积累着能量，向着临界点前进……

丽丽喜悦地感觉到我在家里笑声多了，却没有注意到另外一个变化，这个变化她是不知道的，我在研究所里所见到的笑脸却越来越少了，因为我的工作效率在直线下降。

但是不管怎么说吧，“POT”研究计划已经接近尾声，在这个项目上，我们在世界上还处在领先地位。由于这个原因，我的心情慢慢地又好起来。稿纸在一页一页地翻过去，论文一页一页地厚起来。

又是枫叶流丹的季节了。

秋天，丰硕的秋天，金色的秋天！

I could have another two glasses of it.

Again, she knew what was in my mind. She stretched out her hand to the cupboard and... I couldn't have my meals without her. From that time on, we laughed a lot more at meals. Lily sometimes laughed till she cried.

She worked out that my laughter was directly related to the amount of wine available in the cupboard and she was perfectly satisfied with that.

However, neither she nor I was aware of the trouble which was brewing, the crisis which was building up to flash point...

Lily was delighted to have found out how to keep me happy and cheerful at home but she was in no position to see that things were very different away from home: the smiling faces I met at the institute were getting fewer and fewer for my efficiency at work had dropped sharply.

However, the POT programme was really drawing to a conclusion and our team was leading the world in its field, so I did not worry too much. The pile of papers on my desk was growing higher: I was getting on well with my thesis.

The leaves of the maples began to turn red.

Autumn, the season of plenty, the golden season, had come.

噩　梦

很快就要双喜临门。

一是“POT”研究计划大功告成，二是我和丽丽的结婚纪念日即将到来。

新华社送来了报道“POT”研究计划研究成果的新闻稿，新闻稿里充分地肯定了这项研究工作的重大意义，而且肯定了我个人所做出的贡献。读着这篇稿子时我竟激动得热泪盈眶，因为我想到了那些为这项科学研究甘当人梯、甘当铺路石子的几代科学家所付出的心血，还有那些倒在这条漫长路上的探险者的白骨。

丽丽天天都在望眼欲穿地盼望着这一天。

这一天终于盼到，我又正好赶上休假日。

清晨，太阳刚刚升起，我和丽丽都收拾得漂漂亮亮的，开上汽车，车上还载着轻型快艇，带着精美的野餐，到海滨去了。

天空是那样碧蓝，阳光是那样灿烂。大海是那样温柔，

NIGHTMARE

A double blessing would soon descend upon my house.

One was the imminent end of the POT research programme; the other was the approach of our first wedding anniversary.

Xinhua News Agency sent us a press release, which fully affirmed the great significance of this research project and acknowledged my contribution to it. As I read this press release I found my eyes filled with tears for I was moved by the thought of the painstaking labour by several generations of scientists who were willing to be the stones used to pave the way of this project, and of the bones of those who had died in the course of this long and tortuous journey.

Everyday, Lily was looking forward eagerly to our anniversary.

It came at last and luckily it happened to be my day off.

Very early, just as the sun was rising, we got up and dressed ourselves smartly. We put a light speedboat and some picnic food in the car and drove to the sea.

The sky was blue and the sun was bright. The sea was silky-

细浪是那样缠绵。快艇像箭一样在浪尖上飞驰，我们的笑声和歌声回荡在海面。

微风伸开臂膀把我们拥抱，白云把她细嫩的脸蛋儿贴在我们胸前……

迎着我们的是展翅的海鸥，追着我们的是欢叫的海燕。

饿了，我们在美丽的珊瑚岛上进餐。

困了，我们在暖洋洋的沙滩上睡眠。

直到夕阳钻进暮霭的被窝，鸟儿飞回密林深处，月亮把闪耀的光华洒遍大地，星星眨着好奇的眼睛尾随着与我们做伴，我们才回到自己的家园……

白天，我们只在小岛上吃过一顿野餐，回到家里，都饿了。好在冰箱里什么都有，最重要的是有一位能干的主妇，半小时后，一顿丰盛的晚餐就已经就绪。

我端起酒杯，一股酒香直冲脑际，一看，原来是丽丽悄悄地把葡萄酒换成了浓烈的金奖白兰地，我抬起头来，正迎上她那钻石般的黑眼睛——她正在悄悄地、深情地望着我……

smooth and the ripples played lazily on the sand. The speedboat darted lightly over the surface of the water and the air was filled with our singing and laughter.

A gentle breeze stroked us with warm fingers, and the white cloud seemed to nestle closely to our chest with her tender face...

Around and above us seagulls and petrels swooped and clamoured.

When we were hungry we ate our meal on an enchanting coral island.

When we felt tired we slept on the warm sandy beach.

We didn't go home until the sun had vanished below the horizon and the birds had gone to roost in the thick forest. The moon began shedding her shining light upon the earth and the stars watched us with their curious, sparkling eyes on our way home...

That day we had had only one meal, on the coral island, so we were very hungry when we got home. We had everything for dinner in the refrigerator and the important thing was to have an efficient housewife. Half an hour later a sumptuous dinner was ready.

As I held the wine glass in my hand, a strong smell of wine assailed me, penetrating my head. I looked carefully at the glass and found Lily had quietly replaced the grape wine with a good vintage brandy. I looked up and her shining dark eyes met mine—she was gazing at me calmly and affectionately...

噩梦

什么叫幸福?

什么叫爱情?

那双钻石般闪光的眼睛就是答案。

那双眼睛,

比美酒还要醉人。

因为那眼睛里,

盛满着爱。

我喝了一杯又一杯……

一瓶完了,我让她再取一瓶,今天我要开怀豪饮,痛饮这幸福的满杯!

杯里盛的是幸福,

杯里盛的是青春,

杯里盛的是欢乐,

杯里盛的是爱情!……

这样的杯怎么能停下?

……

我酩酊大醉了。

What did happiness mean?

What did love mean?

Those diamond like bright shining eyes were the answer.

Her eyes intoxicated me more than wine.

For her eyes were full of love.

I drank glass after glass…

When the bottle was empty I asked her to bring another.

That day, I wanted to drink and drink to our happiness.

The glass held the essence of happiness,

The glass held the essence of youth,

The glass held the essence of joy,

The glass held the essence of love! …

Could I stop?...

…

I was dead drunk...

怎么能不醉?

我看到丽丽的脸色变了。她瞅着我的时候，那双眼睛里闪动着恐惧的神色，我才意识到，我大概是醉了。

算了，不喝了，别吓着她，可怜的丽丽!

为了安慰她，我口齿不清地说："我……我……我没碎……我，我……我没睡……"不知怎么的，舌头拐不过弯儿来，这"醉"字老念转音。

我忽然想起我昨天买了一件新鲜玩意儿，是准备送给她的，一高兴，全忘了。这会儿才想起来，那是一只"海市蜃楼"打火机。这种打火机打着以后，它的火焰与燃烧的纸头发生光焰干涉，能变幻出各种各样的幻影和景致。奇妙得不可思议。

我玩给她看，她那个高兴劲儿就别提了，快乐疯了。我让她拿给我纸头，我一张一张地烧给她看，那光焰里有许多古希腊神话中的人物。有华沙美人鱼，有美丽的文艺女神缪斯，有那半截狮身、半截美人的怪物斯芬克斯，还有雷神丘必特和他的儿子火神武尔坎，还有美杜莎，那个

How could I not be?

I noticed Lily's face looked frightened. When she looked at me, there was a fearful look in her eyes. That was when I realized I was drunk.

I should stop now or I would frighten her even more. Poor Lily!

I tried to set her mind at rest by saying indistinctly, "I... am... not... drunk... I... am... not..." I failed to pronounce the word 'drunk' properly.

Suddenly I remembered I had bought a new-fangled gadget the day before as a gift for Lily, but I had been so happy that I had forgotten to give it to her. It was a "Mirage" viewer lighter. It was an exceedingly wonderful plaything: when light shone through it illusions and mirages would appear as a result of the radiation interference generated by the flames of burning paper.

I played with it while she watched. She enjoyed it so much that she wanted to go on and on. I asked her to fetch me some pieces of paper and I lit them, one after another. We saw a lot of ancient Greek mythical figures in the flames; there were the Warsaw Mermaids, the beautiful Muses—goddesses of literature and art, the sphinxes with lions' bodies and women's heads, Cupid, Vulcan the god of fire, and

可怕的蛇发女妖。……可丽丽没看见美杜莎，因为美杜莎出来的时候我用手蒙住了她的眼睛，我告诉她，美杜莎是不能看的，任何人只要看她一眼，就会变成石头。……还有呐，还有更可怕的三首三身的赫加特，她也是个女人，是月亮之神，专门管辖妖魔鬼怪和阴间的亡魂，……她身边是一群群青面獠牙、狰狞可怕的鬼魂幽灵……

丽丽被吓得尖叫起来，依偎在我的身边索索发抖。我把打火机熄掉，幻象没有了。停了一会儿，她忍不住还想看，央求着我。我又打着、烧着纸头，在火与烟雾中又出现了各种各样的幻象。

我看了她一眼，她用双手蒙住眼睛从指头缝里偷着看。

好了，现在登场的不是那些狰狞可怕的鬼怪了，是莎士比亚戏剧《温莎的风流娘儿们》中的那些俏丽的姑娘们了……

我们俩像一对小傻瓜一样，笑着、烧着，烧着、笑着……

我恍恍惚惚地记得，纸头没有了，我叫她打开抽屉，我指指写字台，扔给她钥匙，那里面有的是！……不知为

Medusa, the terrible witch with snake hair... but Lily didn't see Medusa because I covered her eyes with my hand, telling her that anyone who looked at her would be turned into a stone... And there was the even more fearsome Hecate with her three bodies and three heads: she was the goddess of the moon administering demons and ghosts and the souls of the deceased persons underworld...she was surrounded by ghastly green-faced spirits and ferocious long-toothed spectres...

Lilly shrieked with fear and nestled up to me, shivering all over. I turned off the viewer and everything vanished immediately. But after a few minutes she wanted to see them again and pleaded with me to go on, so I lit it up again and fed in more pieces of paper. Amid the flames the apparitions appeared again.

I glanced at her and found she had covered her eyes with her hands and was looking through her fingers.

But it was all right now — the illusions were no longer demons and ghosts but the pretty and captivating characters in Shakespeare's play *The Merry Wives of Windsor*...

We were like two silly children, laughing, burning bits of paper; burning bits of paper, laughing...

I dimly realized that we had burnt up all the paper we had handy. I pointed at the desk and told her to open its drawer as there was a lot of paper in there...I threw her the key...I didn't

什么，取纸的时候……她犹豫了一下，我骂了她一句，她才取了……

我们笑着、烧着，烧着、笑着，直到我头一歪，倒在沙发上睡着了……

understand why she hesitated about fetching the paper from the drawer...Then I shouted at her and she obeyed.

We laughed and burnt sheets of paper and laughed until I couldn't hold out any longer and threw myself down on the sofa and fell asleep...

大 祸

早上一觉醒来，已经是上午8点。

她早已起床，一切都收拾得干干净净。像每天早上一样，枕边放着熨得平平整整的衣服，桌上摆好了热气腾腾的早餐。

吃好早饭，我准备出发上班。

今天是个不平常的日子，也可能这一天将会被历史性地载入史册，因为今天将是“POT”研究计划的研究成果公诸于世的一天。

我拿起皮包，准备神气十足地把“POT”研究计划的论文亲手送交所长，要知道这项成果的公布将会引起国内外的巨大震动，它将宣布：在106号元素与114号元素之间，并非一道海峡，它们当中还有一座小岛——109号元素！

而神奇的109号元素是长寿的，并非有些人所猜测、预言的那样，只能活10^{-14}秒，而且它还将为人类提供巨大的、廉价的、无污染、弱放射的优质能源。

NEMESIS

It was already eight o'clock when I woke up next morning.

Lily was up and had tidied the house. As usual, my clothes were freshly ironed and put by my pillow and steaming hot breakfast was on the table.

After breakfast I was ready to go to work.

Today was a day that might go down in history, for the achievement of the POT research programme would be released for publication.

I picked up my brief case and visualized myself handing in my thesis to the Director in person by putting on grand airs. The announcement of the outcome of this research would produce a massive impact both at home and abroad. It would declare: The area between elements 106 and 114 is not a strait: there is an islet between them—element 109.

The wonderful element 109 was not short-lived, only living for 10^{-14} seconds as predicted, it was long-lived. It would provide mankind with limitless low cost energy, of high quality, non-polluting and weak in radioactivity.

它将意味着核物理的新纪元，它是现代物理学上一块重要的里程碑！

它将宣告，在人类解除了人口危机之后，又解除了能源危机的威胁，它是当代最伟大的科学成就之一。

这是我们109研究室艰苦奋斗了5年的丰硕果实。我是这个研究课题的副组长，组长是我的老师——史纯教授。他逝世后，这个位置始终空缺着，为了纪念他，我们一直没有填补这个空位，就像他还活着一样。

史纯老师，您可以含笑九泉了。

我仿佛已经看到，所有的报纸都在头版头条报道了这个伟大事件。鲜花、贺电、贺信像雪片一样向我飞来。昨天晚上，我一夜做的都是这样的梦。

我将要用……不，是已经用事实证明，所长对我的批评是错误的。我仿佛看到，所长那张像冰封的湖面一样的面孔，终于石破天惊，漾出了层层涟漪……

这些天来压抑在心头的闷气该吐出来了。

我陶醉在甜蜜的想象之中，带着梦幻般的微笑，打开

It was an important milestone in modern physics: it would signal a new era for the physicists.

It would mean that mankind, having resolved the population crisis, could now avert the threat of an energy crisis. It was one of the great scientific achievements of our times.

These were the rich fruits of five years of arduous labour by our Research Section 109. I was the deputy group leader of this research programme, the group leader had been my former teacher, the late Professor Shi Chun. The position of group leader had been vacant since his death, out of respect to his memory, as though he were still alive with us.

Professor Shi Chun, you can now rest content!

I seemed to see the newspaper reports – headlines on the front pages, flowers, congratulatory telegrams and letters pouring into me. I dreamed all this last night.

I would... no, I had proved with facts my supervisor's criticism of me was wrong. I seemed to see his grim and icy face transformed into a face wreathed in smiles...

My pent-up grievances in recent time should be aired.

I was carried away by all these dream scenes with a dreamy smile as I opened my drawer.

了抽屉。我向抽屉里望了一眼，顿时，我像被雷击了一样，呆住了！

一只空抽屉！

这是怎么回事？

我问丽丽，抽屉里的东西哪儿去了？

丽丽被我的脸色吓坏了，话也不会说了。我强作镇静地说："丽丽别害怕，说，文件哪儿去了？"

丽丽吓哭了，她哭着说："不是你昨天晚上一张一张地都烧了吗？"

天哪！我昨天晚上一张一张地都烧了？……让我好好想想。

可不是吗？

昨天真的是一张一张地烧了……

我的全身冷汗直流。

一张一张地烧了……

天哪！

However, when I looked into it, I was dumbstruck as if I were struck by lightning.

It was empty!

How was that? What...?

I asked Lily what she had done with the papers in the drawer.

She was too frightened by my expression to utter a word. I made an effort to appear composed and said, “Lily, don’t be afraid. Tell me where the papers are.”

She burst into tears and said, “Didn’t you burn them up one sheet after another last night?”

Good God! Did I really burn them up one sheet after another last night? ...Let me think it over carefully.

That was exactly what I did.

I did burn them up one by one last night...

I was wet through with cold sweat.

They were burnt up one sheet after another...

Oh my God!

判　决

我被送交特别法庭追究刑事责任。

起诉书中说，那天晚上，我醉后渎职，竟烧掉了国家投资数千万元、我们研究室十多位研究员（教授）、副研究员（副教授）和二十多名研究生、一百多名实验员五年来付出的心血，还有国家从国外以高价买进的十几份专利、技术情报，烧掉了有关109号元素的全部原始记录，其中有实验数据、曲线、照片、记录纸带、报告、全部的档案卷宗。其损失达若干亿元，其中有些损失是无法估计其经济价值的，例如，史纯教授的遗著……

我有何面目见老师于地下！

……天哪，这有多么可怕！

我恨不得把自己的双手剁掉！

那天晚上我为什么没有把我自己烧死！我宁愿给我浑身浇上汽油，把我烧死，也绝不愿意烧掉这些无价之宝、

RETRIBUTION

I was handed over to the special criminal court.

The indictment said that I was derelict of duty after having got drunk that night. I had burnt up all the results of five years' painstaking work by more than ten research fellows (professors) and associate research fellows (associate professors), over twenty graduates and some one hundred laboratory technicians, together with the investment of scores of million dollars by the state in purchasing dozens of patents and technical reports at high price from abroad. I had burnt up all the original records including experimental data, graphs, photographs, transcriptions of tapes, reports and all the files concerning element 109. The loss amounted to several hundred million dollars and some could not even be assessed in terms of economic value, as for instance Professor Shi Chun's work...

The thought of my late teacher...!

...Oh God! How dreadful it was!

My feelings of remorse were so strong that I wished I could chop my hands down...

Why couldn't I have been brunt to death that night? I would rather have been drenched with petrol and burnt to death than to have destroyed those priceless and irreplaceable

稀世之珍！

我被按照过失犯罪从轻判处三年有期徒刑，监外执行。开除公职，留用察看。我被判处罚款的数目20年才能还清。

records.

I was leniently sentenced to three years' imprisonment for committing an unpremeditated crime; the sentence to be performed outside prison. I was also discharged from public employment and placed on probation in the institute. The fine imposed on me had to be paid off in twenty years.

苏　醒

现在，我得好好想一想这一切是怎么造成的。

我像个木头人一样地回到家里。丽丽伏在我身上痛哭，我把她赶了出去。

我把自己关在屋子里，我听得见她趴在地上、扑在门上的啜泣声。可我的心冷得像一块石头。

我的脑子在眩晕、发疼、发麻，我在痛苦地思索着。

我得好好想想……

我把自己关在屋子里，痛苦地思索着。当然，首先是我的责任，我意志薄弱。但是，不正是丽丽解除了我的烟禁，使我的健康越来越坏，控制自己的能力越来越差？是丽丽解除了我的酒忌，使我越来越纵酒狂欢，以至于酿成大祸？不正是她，把葡萄酒换成了白兰地，使我丧失理智，不能自拔？

是她，悄悄地用她那双纤细柔软的手，打开了我一道道枷锁的闸门，把十字路口的绿灯红灯，一股脑儿都换成

AWAKENING

Now, I must think over carefully how all this came about.

I came home in a stupor. Lily tried to creep into my arms, crying her heart out. I drove her outside.

I shut myself in the living room and I could hear that she was crouched on the floor outside, leaning on the door, weeping. But my heart was as hard as stone.

My head was in a whirl, throbbing and aching, but I had to think it all over carefully...bitterly...

I must ponder over it carefully...

Shut up alone in the room, I turned the problem over and over in my mind painfully. I didn't deny that I should bear the main responsibility, and I had been weak-willed. But it was Lily who relaxed my ban on smoking so that my health suffered and my ability to restrain myself was undermined. And it was Lily who encouraged me to drink more so that I indulged myself and made a gross error. It was she who replaced the wine with brandy so that I lost control of myself and...

It was she who stealthily unlocked my doors one by one and turned all the red lights to green on the crossroads with her

绿灯，……多么可怕啊，丽丽！

乍看起来，像是祸生偶然。追本溯源，竟然事出有因，水到渠成。试想想看：要是有天夜晚，所有的铁路、岔道口、机场，一概绿灯齐明，该会有多少车毁人亡，机坠船沉！

事情发生的时候，我是失去理智的，可她是清醒的。

是的，是我命令她从抽屉里取出纸头的。她不会撒谎，这个机器人头脑里没有设计欺骗的程序，她宁可挨打，也不会欺骗，这我是知道的。她也不会记错，她的记忆力像铜鼎上的铭文一样可靠。命令是我发出的，可当时，我是在酩酊大醉之中，可她是清清楚楚的啊！

是的，她只懂得服从，绝对地、无条件地服从。这是在她出生之前就已经为她编排好了的程序，这个程序是那个美国人阿西莫夫制定的。

我想起了环球机器人公司总经理的话：“她简直不是一个独立的人，而是您的身体的延续，像您自己的手脚一样听话。”

不，她比我的手脚还要听话，当时，在我喝醉的时候，

delicate little hands.... Oh, how dreadful it was, Lily!

At first glance it seemed to be an accidental event. However, on closer examination it proved to be by no means accidental. Just think: if all the traffic signals at all the railways, road junctions and airports turned green at the same time on a certain night, how many cars and trains could be destroyed, how many aeroplanes crash and people be killed?

When the accident happened I was befuddled, but she was clear-headed.

True, it was I who ordered her to fetch papers from the desk. She couldn't lie, for her robot's mind was designed without a duplicity programme. She would rather be beaten up than tell a lie. I knew that. She couldn't have remembered it wrong either, for her memory was as infallible as an epigraph inscribed on a copper tripod. The order was issued by me. I was dead-drunk. But she was clear-headed.

Yes, all she knew was obedience, absolute and unconditional obedience. That was a programme designed before she was made, a programme formulated by the American Asimov.

I called to mind the words of the general manager of Universal Robots: "She won't seem like an independent person but simply an extension of your own body. She will serve you like your own hands and feet. "

No, she was more readily at my service than my hands and feet. When I was drunk my hands and feet had betrayed me

我的手脚都已经叛变了，不再服从我的命令，各行其是、各自为政了，可她还在执行我那一道道断送我前程的可怕的命令！

天哪，这太可怕了！

我现在才明白，这种绝对地服从，这种“天仙”般的美丽温柔与顺从有多么可怕，我现在才意识到人的行为在失去鉴别、失去制约的情况下会发生些什么事情！

我曾经为“我们两个人只有一个头脑”而自豪、庆幸。我曾经甚至认为这是构成我美满婚姻的第一要素。现在我才明白，它，正是导致悲剧的原因！

一百个顺从，天哪，我现在才知道它有多么可怕、可憎、可厌！我的事业，我的声誉，我的一切……全都断送在这可怕的“顺从”之中！

我必须离开丽丽，否则下次我还不知会干出些什么事来。亡羊补牢，犹未晚也。

现在我才意识到天然人妻子比机器人妻子好，因为她们有自己独立的见解和思考，她们是一个独立的人，她们不仅懂得应当怎样爱自己的丈夫，而且还懂得应当怎样在

and refused to obey me; they went their own way. But she still carried out my fatal orders to the letter.

Oh, my God, how terrible!

I had now come to understand how dreadful this absolute uncritical obedience, this angelic beauty and tenderness, this submission was. I knew now what a person could do when he lost his ability to distinguish right from wrong and to control himself.

I had rejoiced at us “having one mind” and had even been convinced that it was the first essential of a happy marriage. Now I saw it clearly as a crucial cause of tragedy.

How terrible, hateful and revolting that hundred percent submission was. My career, my reputation, my future ... all were ruined by this dreadful submission.

I must get away from Lily, otherwise I would never know what might happen to me next. Perhaps it was not too late to mend the fold even after some of the sheep had been lost.

Through bitter experience I had come to see that human wives were better than robot wives for they could act and think independently and critically. They were independent persons and they not only loved their husbands but they also

关键时刻制约丈夫的行为。

她们还具有那种令人羡慕的、宝贵的、可爱的、珍珠样的品质——会吵架。

我终于决定把丽丽送回环球机器人公司，如果她不能重新调整数据，学会制约她的丈夫，那就只有一条路：离婚！

凭良心说，丽丽也怪可怜的，她并没有罪，她的心眼儿太好了，她的心地太善良了。有罪的是阿西莫夫，他的三定律固然有合理的内核，却也有可诅咒的缺陷！

knew how to restrain them at the vital moment.

Moreover, they had the inestimable quality, the pearl beyond price—they knew how to quarrel.

Finally I decided to send Lily back to Universal Robots. If they failed to readjust her data to give her the capacity to oppose and restrain her husband, then the only way out would be to divorce her.

In all fairness, Lily was to be pitied. She wasn't to blame. She was made too good-natured and kind-hearted. It was Asimov who was to blame. It is true that his three laws of the robot have rational intentions, but they also have the most accursed defects!

作者简介

魏雅华　中国作家协会会员，陕西省作家协会会员。著名作家，时政经济评论家。

魏雅华曾以《温柔之乡的梦》荣获北京文学奖，以《女娲之石》荣获青春文学奖，以《远方来客》荣获中国科幻小说首届银河奖，以《天火》荣获中国科幻小说第二届银河奖。他还获得了中国海洋文学海燕奖、西安文学奖、中国通俗文学冰熊奖等15项文学大奖。

魏雅华还在网上销售长篇小说多达35部。如长篇小说《裸城》(陕西人民出版社出版),《饥饿》(青海人民出版社出版),《落红》《落枫》《落尘》(新疆人民出版社出版),《媚眼》《白眼》(山东文艺出版社出版),《猫眼》(中国文联出版公司出版),《丽影》(中国戏剧出版社出版),《黑妹》(山东文艺出版社出版)等。长篇纪实文学《病态人格忧思录》(广东经济出版社出版)等。创下多部长篇小说超过20万册的发行量，是著名畅销书作家。

魏雅华是陕西电视台新闻频道《今日点击》栏目评论员，陕西电视台经济频道、西安电视台新闻频道资深评论员。现为专业作家，从事专业的时政、经济评论以及文学创作。

About the author

Wei Yahua is a member of Chinese Writers Association, a member of Shaanxi Writers Association, and a well-known writer and political economic critic.

Wei has won 15 literary prizes in his literary career.

Now there are still 35 of his novels being sold online. He is a well-known best seller writer. Many of his novels have a sales volume amounting to over two hundred thousand copies.

Wei is reviewer for the news channel of Shaanxi TV Station and experienced reviewer for the economic channel of Shaanxi TV Station and Xian TV Station. Now he is engaged in political and economic review as well as literary writing. He is a professional writer.

译者简介

温绍贤 生于香港，早年毕业于中山大学西方语言文学系。温绍贤是资深翻译家和中英文编辑，翻译和译审的书籍超过100部；他还是长期从事英汉语言比较和翻译研究的学者，有多部学术专著问世；他同时又是小说作家，擅长撰写政经历史长篇小说，代表作有《红的回忆》五部曲和“绿印人”系列三部短篇小说集。现任郑州大学西亚斯国际学院荣誉教授。

在中国图书对外推广网和中国作家协会共同建立的“翻译名家”和“作家档案”网上，均有介绍温绍贤的条目。

有关温绍贤生平的详情，请参阅网上“维基百科”对他的介绍。

英文文字编辑简介

蒂娜·巴莱（Tina Bailey），资深英文译审。

About the translator

Wen Shaoxian was born in Hong Kong. He graduated from the Department of Western Languages and Literature at Sun Yat-sen University. He is a veteran translator as well as a professor of translation and comparative grammar. He has translated and copy-edited more than 100 books of different disciplines. Now Wen is honorary professor with SIAS International University in Central China.

Wen is also a literary writer, expert in writing political and historical novels. His representative works include *Red Memories* pentalogy and *New Immigrants*, a series of three short story collections.

About the English copy–editor

Tina Bailey, veteran English copy-editor.